RAILS OF THE
NORTHWEST

THROUGH TIME

DALE PETERKA

AMERICA
THROUGH TIME®
ADDING COLOR TO AMERICAN HISTORY

America Through Time is an imprint of Fonthill Media LLC
www.through-time.com
office@through-time.com

Published by Arcadia Publishing by arrangement with Fonthill Media LLC
For all general information, please contact Arcadia Publishing:
Telephone: 843-853-2070
Fax: 843-853-0044
E-mail: sales@arcadiapublishing.com
For customer service and orders:
Toll-Free 1-888-313-2665

www.arcadiapublishing.com

First published 2018

Copyright © Dale Peterka 2018

ISBN 978-1-63500-072-6

Typeset in Mrs Eaves XL Serif Narrow
Printed and bound in England

INTRODUCTION

The Pacific Northwest encompasses everything from breathtakingly towering mountain ranges to deep canyons to parched deserts occupying a vast stretch of territory extending from the Pacific Ocean east to the Rocky Mountains. Wagons jolting over primitive trails provided the bulk of the initial transportation through this land as Europeans settlement began, though shipping routes did develop on the few rivers with sufficient flow to allow for navigation by shallow drafted riverboats. Railroading in the northwest got its start with a pair of short mule-powered portage tramways built to ferry freight around the Cascade Rapids on the Columbia River forty-five miles east of Portland, the first completed along the north bank in 1851 and a competing line built on the south bank four years later.

The region has always presented a paradox for the railroad industry as it grew beyond it portage roots. Railroad builders encountered innumerable obstacles in pushing rail lines to and then through the Northwest, and the attendant cost structure associated with running trains over steep grades, through heavy snows, and over long distances between major population centers continually tested the railroad companies once they commenced operations. Yet there were vast potential fortunes to be made by successful ventures. Chief amongst these was access to deep water ports on the Pacific coast and the transcontinental flow of trade heading to and from points across the Pacific passing over their docks. The region also represented a major source of traffic by itself, mostly in seemingly endless forests, extensive mineral reserves, and rich loess soils deposited by outwashes from retreating glaciers at the end of the last ice age that proved capable of growing crops of mostly fruit trees and wheat. The Southern Pacific, Union Pacific, Great Northern, Northern Pacific, Milwaukee Road, and Spokane, Portland & Seattle railroads all built major mainlines through the country, along with often dense networks of branchlines spreading out to tap possible traffic sources. Industries and some communities built independent shortline railroads to other places where the big roads could not or would not go.

The railroads themselves played a leading role in developing these resources, and thereby much of the social and economic structure of the region. Several of the railroads received land grants from the Federal government to help finance their construction; the government hoped those lands plus intermingled public lands would be taken up by settlers following the railroads west and put to productive use. The railroads and collaborating development companies wasted no time in occasionally over-advertising the farming potential of the region to nascent farmers, sometimes recruited directly off the docks at Ellis Island, along with others anxious for a new start in a new land. In 1900, railroad financier James J. Hill sold 900,000 forested acres of Northern Pacific Railroad land grants to a group of timbermen led by Frederick Weyerhaeuser, which almost overnight launched one of the largest timber concerns in the nation. The lumber industry grew in leaps and bounds after that point as other established timber operators followed Weyerhaeuser west from the cutover lands of the Great Lakes states. The spectacular scenery especially in the Rockies and Cascade mountain ranges quickly proved to be a major tourist draw, and the railroads played a large role in the creation and development of several national parks to which eastern tourists soon flocked in large numbers, paying top fares for round trip berths in railroad sleeping cars and largely staying at railroad affiliated hotels inside the parks.

In the days before private automobiles and Interstate highways, being on the route of a railroad line more often than not meant the difference between life and death for communities. Several towns left off the railroad route vanished as economic activity moved to the often newly established town by the tracks. Railroads were essential in moving people and commerce, and the train depot became the economic and social centerpiece of almost every town. The railroads themselves became primary economic drivers in many communities, especially in division points that hosted shop complexes, switching yards, and servicing facilities.

The railroad industry today remains an integral part of the northwestern economy, though its importance in the day-to-day lives of the towns through which their trains roll has significantly diminished. While freight traffic is at or near historic levels and commuter rail service has seen dramatic expansions in recent years, long distance passenger service has been reduced to a handful of Amtrak trains on a few select lines. Several mainlines and hundreds of miles of branchlines rendered redundant by corporate mergers or inability to compete have been reduced to biking trails or empty grades returning to nature. Those depots still standing typically house museums or businesses unrelated to the railroad industry, sometimes with the buildings moved to new locations away from the tracks. The steam locomotives, cabooses, and other historic equipment that once captivated public imagination are gone except for a few operating on tourist railroads and museums or relegated to static display pieces in public parks.

Father Dale Peterka has assembled within these pages a wide array of past and present images of railroading in the Pacific Northwest, including glimpses of a few of the practices and technologies the industry used to maintain operations in this land and a good number of the ghosts the ever changing face of the industry has left behind. Take a seat and enjoy this sweeping look at a fascinating piece of American history.

Jeff Moore
Elko, NV

RIDING THE TRAIN: The ride through the Northwest is a magical tour of prairie, mountains, rivers, lakes, and canyons. Best of all, the old-fashioned clickity-clack has yielded to modern welded rail. That sound you hear is the low murmur of steel wheels on seamless rails. *(Great Northern Railway Historical Society archive photo)*

TAKING PICTURES OF TRAINS: One hundred and twenty years ago, when cameras were the size of toasters and primitive film required long exposures, rail photography meant finding subjects that were standing still! At the local roundhouse in Duluth (1911), the shop crew poses with one of the new Mallet locomotives. In Cincinnati on Pete Rose Way (1984), Grand Trunk trainmen share the scene with a diesel engine. *(GNRHS archive photo)*

MINOT DEPOT REDONE: Sometimes time does not march on. It retreats! The Great Northern depot in Minot, North Dakota, was "modernized" in the early 1960s, becoming an ugly stucco box. After fifty years, the railroad and the people of Minot decided that they liked the old look better, and the depot was rebuilt!

THEY CALL ME *HUSTLE MUSCLE*: No one seems to know why the new 3,600 horsepower diesel locomotive, the SD45, needed a moniker, but the first twenty-cylinder, six-axle brute was dubbed *Hustle Muscle* soon after its delivery to the Great Northern. The engine is now over fifty years old and, after twenty-five years of service in Burlington Northern green, is back in its original Omaha orange and Pullman green paint scheme. *(Bob Albano photo)*

AUTO RACKS: In the 1950s, the railroads began shipping automobiles from the factory in specially designed auto-rack cars. Within ten years, enclosures were added to keep the cars from being damaged en route, often by vandals throwing rocks. Hobos would sometimes gain entry and ride in the cars—trashing the interiors along the way! *(Bob Oestreich photo)*

RED CABOOSE: Great Northern caboose X-294 is on roadside display on US-2 at the west end of the Iron Goat Trail at Scenic, Washington. X-294 was built in 1951 and later became part of the Burlington Northern. (A Canadian National caboose is shown in Minnesota.) Cabooses began disappearing from American rails soon after the invention of the end-of-train monitoring device in the 1980s.

GREAT NORTHERN TUNNELS: The 1,458-foot
Cartwright Tunnel, west of Williston and east of
the Montana state line, is the only railroad tunnel
in the state of North Dakota. The tunnel dates
back to 1912 and is now part of a Rails-to-Trails
bike path. At Butte, Montana, abandoned Tunnel
No. 10 featured twenty-foot icicles in 1997. Today
the entire mountainside at Butte—including the
tunnel—has been hauled away to the smelter.

AIR VIEW: From the air, we see the dramatic cliff that gave Cut Bank, Montana its name as well as the impressive steel viaduct that has carried rail traffic on the Great Northern Railway (and its successors) since 1900. Amtrak train No. 8, *Empire Builder*, proudly carries the soubriquet of James J. Hill, founder of the Great Northern and one of the great pioneers of the Northwest.

PRINCE OF WALES HOTEL: Louis W. Hill, son of James J. Hill, became president of the Great Northern in 1908 and began encouraging tourists to visit Montana. He campaigned for the establishing of Glacier National Park in 1910, and the railroad built hiking trails and chalets in remote areas of the park. A pair of magnificent lodges welcomed visitors who wanted to enjoy the mountain scenery without riding a horse all day. Across the border in Canada, Hill built the Prince of Wales Hotel in 1927—in the midst of Prohibition—for American visitors who yearned for cocktails before dinner!

POSING WITH THE POWER: Great Northern Railway Historical Society conventioneers pose with restored steam engine No. 1355 in Sioux City, Iowa, in 2017. The practice of group photography with steam engines goes back to the earliest days of wet-plate film and view cameras. *(Walter Ainsworth collection, PNRA.org)*

LIFE AFTER DEATH: The 4-8-4 class of engine was famous for high speed and power in passenger and freight service. Milwaukee Road engine No. 261 sat outside at the Green Bay museum until 1993 when restoration efforts began. Since then, the big Northern has run 25,000 miles of excursions for its new owners, the Friends of the 261. The earlier photo shows the engine at the museum in 1983. The latter shot was taken in 1999 at Wheeling, Illinois.

ELECTRIC LOCOMOTIVES: In 1915, the Chicago Milwaukee & Puget Sound Railroad put into service a whole fleet of double (back-to-back) electric locomotives on the mountain portion of its Montana mainline. The new locomotives, dubbed boxcabs, were superior in pulling power to anything else on two rails, especially for winter operation in the mountains. Some of them remained in service until the end of the electrification in 1974. *(Walter Ainsworth collection, PNRA.org)* One of two survivors is on display in Duluth, Minnesota.

BOXCAB LOCOMOTIVES: The Milwaukee Road EF-1 boxcabs were built by Alco with General Electric components and ran on 3,000 volts DC accessed from overhead wire. Each unit weighed over 250 tons and developed 3,340 horsepower (as delivered). *(Walter Ainsworth collection, PNRA.org)* The other surviving boxcab is on display in Harlowton, Montana.

BI-POLAR ELECTRIC LOCOMOTIVES: The year 1919 saw the arrival of another kind of electric locomotive on the Milwaukee, the Bi-polar. The design of the new motor was simplicity itself. The motor rotor windings were directly on the axles—no gears. The field windings were encased and mounted on the truck frames. The new design was an immediate success, and the Bi-polars remained in service well into the 1950s. *(Walter Ainsworth collection, PNRA)*

GIANT ELECTRIC LOCOMOTIVE

Used in hauling The Milwaukee Road's famous transcontinental train, The Olympian, over the Cascade Mountains.

The Milwaukee Road is electrically operated over the Belt, Rocky, Bitter Root and Cascade mountains — a distance of 656 miles.

FAST AND POWERFUL: Featured at the Chicago World's Fair in 1933, the great power of the Bi-polars enabled them to pull the Olympic Hiawatha passenger train over the Cascades without helper engines. The public was fascinated! Three different manufacturers of toy trains made scale models of the Bi-polar. *(Walter Ainsworth collection, PNRA)*

LITTLE JOES: In 1947, Soviet Russia ordered a class of electric locomotives from General Electric, but the Iron Curtain came down, and the sale of American locomotives to the Soviets was embargoed. GE was forced to find another buyer for the big motors. The Milwaukee Road bought twelve of them. Dubbed "Little Joes," they arrived in the Northwest just in time to fill in the gaps in the aging Milwaukee electric locomotive fleet. (Walter Ainsworth collection; PNRA)

LAST OF THE LITTLE JOES: When the Milwaukee electrification was removed in 1974, one of the Little Joe's—No. 750, the first one to be purchased—was saved and put on display on the courthouse lawn in Deer Lodge, Montana. In 1998, the electric locomotive was restored and moved from downtown Deer Lodge to the grounds of the nearby Old Prison Museum where it is on display with other railroad relics.

SNOQUALMIE SUBSTATION: There were twenty-two generating substations along the Milwaukee Road electrified zones. Motor-generators inside the buildings converted 100,000-volt AC power coming in from a hydroelectric source on the Missouri River into 3,000-volt DC. When the electrified system was finally shut down, the machinery and most of the buildings were sold. The Snoqualmie substation is gone; two or three others survive. *(Robert Oestreich photo)*

SACAJAWEA HOTEL: The old hotel in Three Forks, Montana dates to the era when people came out from New York or Chicago on the train and took a day of rest from their journey at the fancy hotel right across from the depot. The next day they would board the bus for Yellowstone Park. The inn has been restored and welcomes guests 365 days a year. A first-class dining room is featured. And, they offer champagne at registration! *(Walter Ainsworth collection, PNRA)*

PIPESTONE PASS: Milwaukee Road's many tunnels now stand empty, dark memorials of an age when travelers enjoyed the suspense of passing through the underground darkness on the train. Just east of Butte, Montana, Pipestone Tunnel—2,290 ft. in length, almost a half mile—ran under the Continental Divide. Old US Highway 10 takes you over the top of the pass.

LINE TO LEWISTOWN: A Milwaukee Road branch line ran north from Harlowton into the high prairie country of central Montana, serving mostly farming communities and finally arriving at a first-class train depot in Great Falls. Today, a new short line, Central Montana Rail, serves the area using the original track. Judith River Bridge, damaged in a flood, has been repaired and returned to service. The depot in Great Falls is now an office building.

RYAN DAM: A series of waterfalls once blocked steamboat access between the upper and lower stretches of the Missouri River in Montana. Lewis and Clark had to portage their canoes and equipment around the falls. Today, five massive dams control the flow of the river. The 1,336 ft. Ryan Dam dates back to 1915. It supplied hydropower for the Milwaukee Road electrification.

BUTTE: A Milwaukee Road Baldwin-Westinghouse "quill" locomotive at the depot in Butte, Montana. Passenger service to Butte was discontinued in 1957 and the depot became the location for station KFLX studios. The building underwent a major restoration in the 1970s. *(Walter Ainsworth collection, PNRA)*

MISSOULA: Farther west, the Milwaukee Road depot in Missoula, Montana has been restored and today serves as national headquarters for the Boone and Crockett Club and offices of the University of Montana. *(Walter Ainsworth, Mitch Goldman photos)*

CROSSING THE COLUMBIA: At Beverly, Washington, the Milwaukee Road crossed the mighty Columbia River on a two-million-dollar bridge. Since there were no roads in the region, bridge construction materials were brought in on steamboats. The bridge took two years to build. At the west end of the bridge, westbound trains encountered the bleak Saddle Mountains. Today's visitor finds only an abandoned bridge in the windswept wilderness. *(Walter Ainsworth, Robert Oestreich photos)*

AT RENSLOW ON INTERSTATE 90:
The 678-ft. Milwaukee Road bridge at Renslow, Washington, predates the interstate highway running beneath it. Much of the Milwaukee roadbed west of here into the Cascades is now open to hikers and bikers, but the bridge itself is off-limits. There are plans to reopen it. *(Robert Oestreich photo)*

YAKIMA CANYON: North from Ellensburg, Washington, the Milwaukee Road shared the canyon of the Yakima River with the Northern Pacific Railroad, which had arrived in the Northwest twenty-five years earlier. Today, the Milwaukee roadbed through the canyon is the John Wayne Trail. The Northern Pacific rails on the near side of the river are used by the BNSF. *(Robert Oestreich photos)*

AMTRAK AT HYAK: In December 1977, the word went out on the railfan jungle telegraph that the line over Stampede Pass had been blocked by snow and that Amtrak's *Empire Builder* would be detouring on the Milwaukee Road over Snoqualmie Pass—accessible on Interstate 90 even in winter. Robert Oestreich and Casey Adams were among serious rail photographers who ventured out to capture the rare shot. *(Robert Oestreich photos)*

EMERGING FROM EAST PORTAL:
The Milwaukee's 11,894-ft. Snoqualmie Tunnel at the summit of the Cascades is open, but hikers and bike riders are advised to walk through the bore with flashlights and to wear warm clothing! Before the abandoned roadbed became the John Wayne Trail, the only traffic through Snoqualmie Tunnel was the vehicles used by the scrappers who removed the rails and ties.

BANDARA BRIDGE: In 1974, in the last days before the Milwaukee Road abandoned its Western Extension, Bob Oestreich made the long climb from the Garcia turnoff to the overlook above the Bandara Bridge to photograph one of the last freights over Snoqualmie Pass. *(Bob Oestreich photo)*

HALL'S CREEK: The bridge over Hall's Creek west of the tunnel was damaged by slash and debris washing down from the hillside and accumulating against the trestle legs. Today, the gap has been repaired, and the bridge is open once again as part of the John Wayne Trail. *(Walter Ainsworth collection, PNRA)*

LOGS AND LOG CARS AT TACOMA: In 1909, the Milwaukee Road arrived on the West Coast to find that the Northern Pacific and the Great Northern had signed up most of the firms shipping goods back east, but the market for forest products was massive in those days, and the Milwaukee soon found itself in the business of shipping logs to the mills and lumber to the markets. *(Bob Oestreich photos)*

ST. PAUL UNION DEPOT: Northern Pacific passenger train turning away from the Mississippi River as it departs St. Paul Union Depot. At Northtown, it will turn west to reach Fargo, Billings, Spokane, and Seattle. Diesels took over in the mid-1950s. *(Walter Ainsworth collection, PNRA)*

HIGH LINE BRIDGE: The 3,860-ft. Valley City Bridge in North Dakota was built by the Northern Pacific Railroad in 1908. Located about sixty miles west of Fargo, the bridge is an important feature on the Burlington Northern Santa Fe Railway (BNSF). When trains use the bridge, the rumble of their wheels can be heard all over town! A BNSF excursion crossed with Milwaukee Road engine No. 261 in 1998.

BRIDGE AT BISMARCK: The Northern Pacific Railroad completed the Missouri River Bridge at Bismarck in 1882. Before then, according to the stories, the cars had to be ferried across the river—except in winter, when rails were laid on the frozen river and traffic rolled across on the ice! The present spans were put in place in 1905. The bridge carries over a dozen trains a day. There are rumors that it will be replaced.

NP STEEL AND WOODEN CABOOSES: Northern Pacific cabooses are preserved and on display in South Heart, North Dakota, and Livingston, Montana. A brakeman riding in the caboose—the last car on the train—would walk back with a flag to warn following trains if the train made an unscheduled stop. When he was ready to resume the trip, the engineer would call the brakeman back to his caboose with a few toots on the whistle!

SULLY SPRINGS, NORTH DAKOTA: An excursion train rolls through the badlands of North Dakota behind ex-Milwaukee Northern No. 261. Colonel George Armstrong Custer and the Seventh Cavalry followed this same route across North Dakota on their way to the Little Big Horn in 1876. After a new connector was put in, the Northern Pacific mainline became a major route for low-sulfur coal moving to eastern markets from Wyoming.

QUILL DRIVE LOCOMOTIVE: President Warren Harding poses in the locomotive cab of Milwaukee Road quill locomotive No. 10305. Soon after the arrival of the General Electric boxcabs, the Milwaukee Road took delivery of ten Baldwin-Westinghouse electric locomotives for high-speed passenger work. The nickname "quill" was inspired by the locomotive axles, which were encased in separate hollow shafts. The traction motors drove the hollow sleeves, or quills, and torque was transferred to the drive wheels by finger extensions. *(Walter Ainsworth collection, Library of Congress collection)*

STATION-STOP IN LIVINGSTON: In the 1970s, Amtrak took the southern route through Montana and stopped at half a dozen cities on the old Northern Pacific mainline. Among them was Livingston, a major servicing point for the old NP and the site of Livingston Shops. A first-class depot was built in 1902—now the Yellowstone Gateway Museum—and survives under the protection of the Livingston Depot Foundation. *(Oestreich photo)*

BOZEMAN PASS, ELEVATION 5,702 FT.: The railroad dug a 3,000-ft. tunnel under Bozeman Pass in 1884. In 1945, the old tunnel was closed, and a new Bozeman Pass tunnel was completed. Interstate 90 provides access to both ends of the tunnel for photographers. *(Warren McGee photo, Walter Ainsworth collection, PNRA)*

THE BUTTE LINE: Northern Pacific's *North Coast Limited* rounds the curve at Welch, Montana approaching the Continental Divide on Homestake Pass. At the time of publication of this book, the rails are still in place on Homestake Pass, but there has not been a train through there since 1983. *(Warren McGee color photo, William Kuebler collection) (double header from Walter Ainsworth collection PNRA)*

WHEN MEN WORE HATS: The citizens of Helena, Montana were delighted when the first train rolled into town in 1883, and train travel to the east and west coasts became available. The Northern Pacific depot in Helena is still a busy railroad center, but Montana Rail Link is the new name on the door. Amtrak discontinued service to Helena in1981. In June 1956, the Northern Pacific Railroad donated their ten-wheeler No. 1382 for display at the depot in Helena, Montana, where it remains today in good condition.

STEAM ENGINE STUFFED AND MOUNTED: In western states, it is common to encounter a steam locomotive on display in a park or at the depot. Among the many Northern Pacific engines that have been saved is a ten-wheeler in Missoula and a Pacific in Bismarck.

THE NORTHERNS: One of the great locomotive designs of the 1920s was known as the Northern. Named for the Northern Pacific, and the first railroad to use the 4-8-4 wheel arrangement, the "Northerns" successfully combined power, strength and stability. Ten years later, a new kind of locomotive was being exhibited, and the handwriting was on the wall! In the space of a generation, steam engines would disappear from America's mainlines; diesel would be king! *(Photos by Ron Nixon; Walter Ainsworth collection, PNRA)*

SKYLINE TRESTLE: West of Helena, at the foot of the Continental Divide, the railroad encountered a major barrier that required a major structure. Austin Creek Canyon had steep sides and tight confines. Only a curved bridge across the entrance of the canyon would do. Called Skyline Trestle, the Northern Pacific bridge is 94 ft. high and 494 ft. in length. It still carries a dozen trains over the divide every day.

MULLAN PASS: Today a gravel road leads from Skyline Trestle up the hill to Mullan Pass and the Continental Divide—a lonely drive! One hundred and fifty years ago, the spot was a busy crossroads! Lieutenant Mullan's Road crossed the Rockies at this spot on its way from Fort Benton, Montana to Fort Walla Walla, Washington. When the railroad came through in 1883, they dug the 3,896-ft. Blossburg tunnel under the pass. *(Montana Historical Society, Helena)*

MISSOULA DEPOT: The Northern Pacific depot in Missoula, Montana, was used by the NP from 1901 to 1971, when passenger service was taken over by Amtrak. After 1979, Amtrak no longer served Missoula. A restaurant now occupies part of thc building. *(Walter Ainsworth collection, PNRA)*

MARENT: The original mainline of the Northern Pacific west of Missoula left the Clark Fork Valley to climb over a divide to the Flathead River. On the way up the divide, the rails encounter the spectacular Marent Trestle. The original 222-ft. bridge at this site (1883) was made from wood; an iron bridge replaced it two years later. Modern steel replacement trusses were installed in 1927 and are still in use by the Montana Rail Link. *(Walter Ainsworth, Mike Biehn photos)*

SAINT REGIS: At St. Regis, Montana the Northern Pacific low level freight line reversed direction following the Clark Fork River to link up with the original mainline at Paradise, Montana after a long detour. The Milwaukee Road mainline used to cross the river and the NP at St. Regis on a steel bridge and continue west up into St. Paul Pass. Today, the bridge is gone, and the Milwaukee roadbed has become the Olympian Trail. The Montana Rail Link still carries daily freight trains on the old NP.

LOOKOUT PASS: The Northern Pacific built a branch line west from St. Regis to gain access to the mines in Kellogg and Wallace, Idaho. The climb over Lookout Pass was a steep one, with wooden trestles, a tunnel, and hairpin turns. Today the roadbed is the Northern Pacific Hiking Trail, and articulated locomotives on the hill are a distant memory. *(Henry Griffiths photo, author's collection)*

WALLACE DEPOT: The Interstate 90 through the town of Wallace, Idaho, was the last stretch to be completed. When the highway came through, the narrow canyon made it necessary to move the impressive NP depot out of the way of progress. Today the building is nearby, in spotless condition! *(Bob Kelly, Mitch Goldman photos)*

Two More Cabooses: The red NP caboose on display at Bangor, Wisconsin, is an older design and was made from wood. The blue Montana Rail Link caboose at Glendive, Montana in 1998 shows modern caboose design: steel body and underframe. Montana was one of the last states to require cabooses on mainline freight trains.

SANDPOINT, IDAHO: In north Idaho, the Northern Pacific Railroad encountered beautiful Lake Pend Oreille. Pressed in by canyon walls on two sides, the only way through was to build the railroad across the water, which they did on a spectacular water-level trestle nearly two miles long. The original wooden bridge of 1884 had a draw span to allow steamboats to pass; pleasure craft can still slip thorough the opening in the causeway today. (*Walter Ainsworth, Sean Kelly photos*)

ELLENSBURG: After crossing the central Washington wilderness, the railroad reached the welcome sight of Ellensburg, the Yakima Canyon and the approach to the Cascade Mountains. In 1981, the Northern Pacific *North Coast Limited* no longer ran, but the Ellensburg depot was still in use by Amtrak. Major depot restoration was completed in 2015. *(Walter Ainsworth collection, PNRA)*

YAKIMA CANYON: Eons ago, the Yakima River carved a deep canyon into the east slope of the Cascades, allowing the Northern Pacific, and later the Milwaukee Road, to run their rails well up into the mountains without serious barriers. Both railroads required major tunnels at the top of the ridge, but Yakima Canyon was a relatively easy route from Ellensburg most of the way up. (*Oestreich photos*)

STAMPEDE TUNNEL: The Northern Pacific Railroad finally arrived on the Pacific Coast—at Portland, Oregon! At first, a humble branch line from Portland served Tacoma and Seattle. In 1888, the Northern Pacific tunnel at Stampede Pass was finally completed and the NP mainline from Yakima finally reached Puget Sound. The name "Stampede" was the moniker given to the pass when some of the early workers at the site were fired for poor performance and were sent away without pay or provisions! *(Walter Ainsworth, Bob Oestreich photos)*

GREEN RIVER TRESTLE: The Northern Pacific trestle at Lester, Washington was a landmark on the western slope of the Cascades at the headwaters of the Green River. From here, it was downhill all the way to the Pacific Ocean. *(Walt Ainsworth and Bob Oestreich photos)*

LESTER DEPOT AND SCOUTS: The old Northern Pacific depot and tower at Lester was later destroyed by arsonists, but the Boy Scouts touring Stampede Pass with scoutmaster Jim Frederickson never forgot their visit to the "Mainstreet of the Northwest". *(Northern Pacific archive photos)*

BUTTE ANACONDA & PACIFIC BOXCABS: Butte, Montana, was called "the richest hill on earth." Silver mines fostered early development, but veins of copper were later discovered and quickly became the source of greater interest. The ore was hauled twenty-six miles to Anaconda where water was available for refining. The Butte Anaconda & Pacific Railroad began in 1892. In 1913, the railroad put up overhead wire and bought electric box-cab locomotives for more efficient transport of copper ore. *(Montana Historical Society photo archive)*

SILVERBOW CANYON: At Durant, Montana the newcomer BA&P Railroad crossed over the mainline of the Northern Pacific in Silverbow Canyon. Later, in 1909, the Milwaukee Road mainline came through Durant as well. The dramatic old black-and-white photo of the three railroads at Durant was one-of-a-kind. Today, Montana Rail Link still uses the old NP tracks. The BA&P became the Rarus Railroad in 1985. In 2007, its name was changed to Butte Anaconda & Pacific once again.

PORTLAND: The spectacular Union Station in Portland, Oregon, with its 150-ft. tower, underwent a major renovation on its hundredth anniversary in 1996. Today, it serves Amtrak and local rail service, and contains offices and a restaurant. *(Oestreich photo)*

ENGINE 700: Spokane Portland & Seattle No. 700 was retired and placed on display in a local park in Portland in 1958. In 1990, it was restored to service and ran several excursions. Its last run was in 2006. Today it is on display at the new Oregon Rail Heritage Center in Portland. (Walter Ainsworth collection, PNRA)

FALLBRIDGE: The first shot shows the Celilo Bridge before the Dalles Dam was built on the Columbia River. The bridge dates to 1912. This was Celilo Rapids, where generations of Native American Indians fished for salmon. Note the difference in water level and the need for a draw span at the south end of the bridge for riverboat passage. Lewis and Clark came through Celilo in 1805. The Oregon Trunk line still carries BNSF traffic in competition with the Union Pacific line running south from Portland. *(Walter Ainsworth collection, PNRA)*

WISHRAM: The little railroad town of Wishram
features the former Spokane Portland & Seattle
(SP&S) rail yard, the Celilo bridge across the
Columbia, a tunnel just east of town, and a
Great Northern steam locomotive on display
near the depot! *(Walter Ainsworth, Jean-Marc
Frybourg photos)*

RAILROAD TOWN: Wishram, Washington, was a junction of the Spokane Portland & Seattle mainline and the Oregon Trunk line coming up through central Oregon from California. Wishram is still a busy junction today, but the Burlington Northern Santa Fe is now the proud owner of both lines. (*Walter Ainsworth, Stu Levene photos*)

CAPE HORN: At a spot aptly called Cape Horn, the rails of the Spokane Portland & Seattle Railway required some serious tunneling to get through the rock formations that crowded right up against the north shore of the mighty Columbia. *(Walter Ainsworth collection, PNRA, Bob Oestreich photos)*

BEACON ROCK: Originally named Castle Rock by Lewis and Clark, Beacon Rock is the number one landmark on the Columbia River. In 1916, Henry Biddle and Charles Johnson bought the 680-ft. rock from the state of Washington and spent three years building a path to the summit. Spectacular! From the summit, you can watch the train traffic on the BNSF mainline below. *(Walter Ainsworth collection, PNRA)*

VANCOUVER DEPOT: The old SP&S depot in Vancouver, Washington, on the north side of the Columbia, still watches over the spot where trains from Portland and Seattle meet. The line to the left heads upriver to Pasco and Spokane. *(Walter Ainsworth + Richard Suggs photos)*

BURR CANYON BRIDGE: The SP&S mainline heading east from Pasco to Spokane had to make the tough climb out of the Snake River Gorge. On the way out, it crosses a great steel trestle at lonely Burr Canyon. The old railroad roadbed is now the Columbia Plateau Trail. *(Ainsworth, Oestreich photos)*

COLUMBIA GORGE: The Portland section of the Amtrak *Empire Builder*, as it did in the days of the Great Northern, follows the Columbia River through some remarkable scenery. At Spokane, the section from Portland joins the section from Seattle for the remainder of the trip across Montana and North Dakota to St. Paul and Chicago. *(Oestreich photo)*

UNION PACIFIC: Union Pacific engineer Bob Krieger in the cab of No. 844. In 1994, the Union Pacific Railroad ran an excursion train from Baker City, Oregon to Spokane. At Hinkle, Oregon the steamer No. 3985 was cut off the train in favor of diesels. No 3985 stayed behind to pose for photographs with an old truck. The railfans were delighted!

EARLY LOCOMOTIVE DESIGN: The first 4-4-0 locomotives in the US were so successful that some of them stayed in service for fifty years! The National Park Service built duplicates of the Promontory engines for display at the Gold Spike National Historic Site in Utah. The Northern Pacific saved one of their American Standards at Bonanzaville in Fargo, North Dakota.

STEEL BRIDGE: The great Joso Trestle at Lyons Ferry, Washington was built between 1910 and 1912 and spans the Snake River, giving the Union Pacific Railroad access to Spokane and the Canadian border from eastern Oregon. Union Pacific E9s were used for this segment of the 1994 excursion.

AMTRAK LOCOMOTIVES: Amtrak used old hand-me-down locomotives in its first few years, then purchased 150 new SDP40s. In 1975, when the new units caused a series of derailments, the company switched to the F40s. Very successful, the F40s served as their mainline power for almost twenty years. *(Oestreich photo)*

THE CITY OF PORTLAND: For many years, the Union Pacific *City of Portland* ran from Chicago out to Cheyenne, Pocatello, Boise, over the Blue Mountains into Oregon and down to Portland along the Columbia River—some of the best scenery in the West! *(Oestreich photo)*

DINNER IN THE DINER, NOTHING COULD BE FINER: People always put the meals in the dining car at the top of their list of favorite experiences on the train. This has been especially true on the long-distance runs, where the railroads tended to show off their best menus and their best service. *(GNRHS archive photo)*

DOME CAR: It was after the Second World War that the railroad began to introduce cars with glass overhead windows for viewing the mountains of the West. Only a few of the old dome cars survive today, mostly in private ownership, but Amtrak's club cars have gone a step further with glass overhead and windows clear down to ankle level! *(GNRHS archive photo)*

SEMAPHORES: Here's how they controlled train traffic in the good old days! When the semaphore blade was up, the line ahead was clear and open. When the blade was sideways, the command was "stop!" *(Robert Oestreich photos)*

KING STREET STATION: Seattle's train depot is located in the Pioneer Square section of downtown Seattle. King Street Station welcomed the Great Northern and Northern Pacific passenger trains beginning May 10, 1906. In 1971, Amtrak arrived. *(Azahel Curtis photo; Walter Ainsworth collection; PNRA)*

BUFFALO: Hunted nearly to extinction in the nineteenth century, bison can be found today in a dozen prairie states. This herd is located west of Browning, Montana. The bison are thriving under the care of the Blackfeet people! Just west of Havre is the "buffalo jump" where Indians used to stampede the big animals over a cliff.

CAMAS PRAIRIE: The Camas Prairie in central Idaho is like an American Shangri-La: an area of wheat fields and small towns surrounded—and isolated—by mountain barriers on three sides and Hells Canyon on the fourth. Headed for Lewiston, Idaho, a short freight train is dwarfed by the massive Snake River Canyon in 1994. Wonders lie ahead! *(Walter Ainsworth collection; PNRA)*

HALF MOON BRIDGE: Today, the spectacular Half Moon Bridge on the Camas Prairie Railroad remains visible on the hillside south of Lewiston, Idaho. Built in 1907, the bridge is 141 ft. high and 684 ft. long. A dozen wooden trestles on the mainline give the railroad its nickname. *(Walt Ainsworth collection PNRA)*

CAMAS PRAIRIE RAILROAD: A hundred years ago, the Union Pacific Railroad and the Northern Pacific teamed up to build a line into Camas Prairie. The railroad was dubbed "the railroad on stilts" for the many wooden trestles that carried the rails. The 1975 movie *Breakheart Pass* was filmed on this line. *(Montana Historical Society archive photo)*

COTTONWOOD TRESTLE: The Camas Prairie was operated, alternately one year at a time, by the Union Pacific and the Northern Pacific. Traffic was mostly grain and lumber. The line closed in 2002. All of the bridges survive but one.

iaduct across Lawyer's Canyon, Idaho.
286 feet high, 1580 feet long.

STEEL INSTEAD OF STILTS: In Idaho's land of wooden bridges, there was one exception, the great steel viaduct over Lawyers Creek—296 ft. in height—which stands today abandoned, as does the entire line!

ROTARY PLOW: The rotary plow was invented by a Canadian, J. W. Elliot, in 1869. Rotary plows used in the US were built by Cooke Locomotive & Machine Works of Patterson, New Jersey. Today, rotaries are rarely used in the US, as they are expensive to operate and prone to damage from rocks and other debris mixed with the snow. In Canada, it's a different story! *(Walter Ainsworth collection; PNRA)*

OBSOLETE TODAY: Rotary plows are on display at Chama, New Mexico, on the Cumbres & Toltec Scenic Railroad. Others can be seen at North Freedom, Wisconsin and in Maple Valley, Washington. In Canada, on the other hand, they can still be seen in action! *(GNRHS and Bob Kelly photos)*

SNOW SHEDS: The first snow sheds were built in California in 1870 to protect the transcontinental line over Donner Pass. In a region full of trees, the logical material for those early sheds was wood. Later, the invention of reinforced concrete introduced a new and stronger type of cover. The concrete shed at Tye, Washington, is over 100 years old! *(Oestreich photo)*

OREGON TRUNK: The simultaneous efforts of the Great Northern and the Union Pacific to build lines from the Columbia River following the Deschutes River into the interior of Oregon led to the so-called Deschutes River War, with violent encounters along the way. The story makes good reading! (*Walt Ainsworth and John Biehn photos*)

WILLOW CREEK TRESTLE: The Willow Creek Bridge is located in Madras, Oregon. It's 1,050 ft. long and 275 ft. high. It dates to 1911 and is still in daily use. *(Walter Ainsworth collection; PNRA)*

CROOKED RIVER: One of the unsung marvels of the twentieth century is the bridge at Metolius, Oregon. For over a hundred years, it has carried heavy railroad traffic across the Crooked River Gorge. *(Walter Ainsworth collection; PNRA)*

AMERICA'S ONCE HIGHEST BRIDGE: At 320 ft. above the water, the Crooked River Bridge was the highest railroad bridge in the US when it was built. *(Water Ainsworth collection, PNRA)*